For Miranda S.H.
For my wife Jean J.W.

Published 1981 by Methuen Children's Books Ltd,
11 New Fetter Lane, London EC4P 4EE
in association with
Walker Books, 17–19 Hanway House,
Hanway Place, London W1P 9DL

Text © 1981 Walker Books
Illustrations © 1981 Juan Wijngaard

First printed 1981
Printed and bound in Italy by Sagdos SpA

British Library Cataloguing in Publication Data
Hastings, Selina
  Sir Gawain and the Green Knight
  I. Title   II. Gawain-poet
  III. Sir Gawain and the Green Knight. *Adaptations*
  823'.9'14 (J)   PZ7.H2813/

  ISBN 0–416–05860–4

Sir Gawain and the Green Knight

Words by Selina Hastings

Illustrations by Juan Wijngaard

METHUEN/WALKER BOOKS

London · Sydney · Auckland · Toronto

IT WAS CHRISTMAS, and King Arthur and his knights of the Round Table were at Camelot. For a full fifteen days there had been feasting and jousting, music and dancing. On the first day of the New Year, the King himself led the dance with Guinevere his Queen. At dinner, according to custom, he insisted that everyone be served before he would sit down. He announced that he would not eat until he had heard some tale of great adventure.

Hardly had he spoken, his voice clear above the talking and laughter and sound of trumpets, when there rode into the hall a terrifying figure – a giant of a man, massively built, whose vast limbs, even his hair and beard, were a brilliant green. He wore a green tunic and from his shoulders hung a richly embroidered cloak trimmed with green fur and studded with emeralds. The saddle and bridle of his horse were of green leather, its mane and tail plaited with green silk. Holding in one hand a branch of holly and in the other a huge axe, the green giant rode up to the banqueting table.

'Which of you is the King?' he demanded.

Nobody moved. The entire company was speechless with astonishment at this unearthly apparition.

Arthur was the first to recover. 'I am the King,' he said courteously. 'And I invite you to join our feast.'

'I cannot stay,' replied the Knight. 'I have come to challenge you and your knights – by repute the bravest men in Christendom. Is there any man bold enough to exchange blows with me?'

He paused for a moment, then continued. 'The rules are that he aim a blow at me now with this axe. In exactly one year's time he must allow me to return that blow.'

No one spoke.

The Knight looked around, surprised. 'What!' he exclaimed. 'Are these the famous knights of the Round Table, and not one of you dares give me an answer?'

Arthur, stung by the contempt in the stranger's voice, leaped to his feet. 'The game you propose is foolish,' he said. 'But I will take you on. Give *me* your axe.'

Then Gawain, the youngest of the knights, stood up. 'Sire, please let me take up this challenge. I have not yet had a chance to prove myself. I beg you to grant me this favour.'

'Noble Gawain,' replied Arthur, 'take the axe. Strike your blow boldly.'

'A noble opponent indeed!' exclaimed the Green Knight, dismounting from his horse. 'Sir Gawain, you must swear that in exactly one year and a day you will seek me out and allow me to return your blow.'

'I give you my word,' said Gawain.

Then the Green Knight knelt at Gawain's feet, bowing his head so that his neck was plainly exposed. Gawain lifted the axe up high and brought it whistling down, severing the Knight's head cleanly from his shoulders.

The head rolled on the floor, blood spurting from the wound, but the Knight never faltered. Rising to his feet, he picked up his head and, tucking it under his arm, swung himself up into the saddle.

As he passed Gawain, the head turned and regarded him solemnly. 'Remember your promise, Gawain. Meet me at the Green Chapel in one year and a day.' Then spurring his horse, the Green Knight galloped out of the hall.

Nearly a year passed and the time came for Gawain to leave Camelot in search of the Green Chapel. With a heavy heart, he took leave of Arthur and his court. All the knights and their ladies came to wish him well, many of them afraid that they would never see him again.

At dawn the next day, Gawain called for his armour. A crimson carpet was laid before him and on it were heaped his arms, brightly polished and ornamented with gold. Two pages knelt before him to hand him first his doublet of silk and his fur-lined coat. Then they fastened on his steel shoes and buckled on to his legs the gleaming cuisses and greaves with their golden hinges. Next came the breastplate and gauntlets, then his spurs and the great sword which hung from his waist on a silken belt. Lastly they gave him his helmet, and his shield with the holy symbol, the star-shaped Pentangle, painted on it.

Gawain's horse, Gringolet, was standing ready harnessed for the Knight to mount. The charger looked magnificent with his scarlet saddle fringed with gold, his bridle embroidered with gold and coloured silks.

Brandishing his shield, Sir Gawain drove his spurs into Gringolet's side and the sparks flew from the horse's hooves as they struck the cobblestones of the castle yard.

So Gawain set off on his great adventure. The country through which he rode was wild and in the grip of a harsh winter. The sky was dark with snow and the roads hard as iron. At night he half froze to death, and during the day the rain came down in icy sheets on his cold armour. Often he had to sleep in the open, as he passed few dwellings where he could ask for shelter. He met no one who could direct him to the Green Chapel.

He rode for many miles through unknown country and at every turn found himself challenged to fight. At every river he crossed, at every mountain pass through which he made his way, there he found some terrible monster blocking his path. He battled almost to the death with fire-breathing dragons, fought with packs of starving wolves, did battle against tribes of trolls who lived in caves high up among the crags. He was attacked by bears and wild boar and by hideous ogres who lay in wait for him as he rode through forest paths and across the open, unprotected fells.

And yet Gawain suffered less from these constant trials of strength and courage than from the pitiless winter. His clothes froze to his skin and the metal of his sword and shield were too cold to touch. Snow piled high in soft white drifts on either side of him and icicles hung from the blackened branches of the trees.

By Christmas Eve Gawain had almost lost hope. In despair he prayed to the Virgin Mary, begging her to help him.

The next morning he came upon a castle in the middle of a wood. It was the most magnificent castle Gawain had ever seen, its turrets and battlements gleaming through the bare trees, pennants fluttering gaily from the gilded towers. His spirits rising, Gawain called to the keeper of the gate. 'Good sir, will you ask the lord of this castle if I may shelter here for the night?'

Within minutes the drawbridge was lowered. A squire led Gringolet to the stables while two servants unbuckled Gawain's armour, and then escorted him to his host, who was waiting to greet him in front of a blazing fire.

Sir Bercilak was a tall, thickset man with a bushy red beard. 'Sir Knight, you are welcome,' said he, clasping Gawain in his arms. 'I beg you to treat this castle and everything in it as your own!' Then he showed Sir Gawain to a luxuriously furnished room in which was a great bed curtained in heavy brocade. Here he gave him robes of velvet and ermine, before leading him back to the fire where, seated on quilted cushions, they dined off spiced meats and the finest wine.

At midnight Bercilak, accompanied by his pretty wife, took his guest to hear Mass. The lady, while kneeling apparently in prayer, could not take her eyes off the handsome young man. She peeped at him through her fingers, glancing at him from beneath her eyelashes when she thought he was looking the other way.

Eventually her curiosity got the better of her and she slid out from her pew and came up to the Knight. She had with her an old woman as squat and ugly, as stout and wrinkled, as she herself was slender and beautiful.

Gawain bowed politely to the older woman, then gazed in rapture at her lovely companion, marvelling at her clear skin and brilliant colouring, her graceful figure and perfect features. He was brought out of his trance by the lady's husband, who, taking him gently by the arm, offered him a cup of mulled wine with which to drink his health before retiring.

For the next three days Gawain was lavishly entertained. On the fourth day he announced that he must leave, explaining that he had to find the Green Chapel.

The lord laughed when he heard this. 'If that be the case, you can stay here. The Green Chapel is barely two miles from this castle. Stay until New Year and enjoy yourself!' Gawain was delighted and accepted eagerly.

'You have had a long and tiring journey,' his host continued. 'It is important that you rest to prepare for your forthcoming ordeal. In the morning I shall go hunting, but I suggest you remain in the castle and lie in bed as long as you like. My wife will entertain you. And let us make a bargain: on my return at night, I will give you whatever I have got in the chase in exchange for whatever you have won during the day here.'

The next day Bercilak and his retinue left at dawn while Gawain lay sleeping until nearly midday. He was awakened by a tiny noise. With one eye he saw the door slowly open and the lady of the castle tiptoe towards his bed. Embarrassed, Gawain pretended to be asleep. The lady came closer, then sat on the end of the bed and watched him intently, waiting for him to wake. After a while, realising she had no intention of leaving, Gawain opened his eyes, exclaiming with astonishment at seeing her there.

'Good morning, Sir Gawain,' said the lady, laughing prettily. 'How deeply you sleep!'

'Madam, good morning,' replied Gawain as formally as he could from the depths of his bed.

'I have come to entertain you,' she continued roguishly. 'I shall keep you in bed and you must do whatever I say, for I hear you are known throughout Christendom for your honour and courage, and this is my only chance to have such a famous Knight to myself.' She looked at him archly. 'I am here to please you,' she said. 'You have only to ask and I will bring anything you desire.'

'Madam,' stammered Gawain, 'you are very kind. I am certainly not the hero you describe. But if there is any honourable way in which I can serve you, I will be proud to do so.'

'Most ladies I know would rather have love than brave deeds,' she said softly, lowering her eyes.

'Madam, your husband, my host . . . I cannot betray his trust. But if you will accept me as your champion, I will dedicate myself to your service.'

The lady pouted and looked away for a moment. Then she smiled and, taking his hand in both her own, chattered on of this and that, praising Gawain's prowess until at last, to his relief, she got up to go.

'Surely a man as renowned for gallantry as you would not let a lady leave without a kiss?' she whispered.

'I am at your command,' replied Gawain, brushing her cheek lightly with his lips.

That evening the hunting party returned, triumphantly displaying as their prize a magnificent stag. 'This is yours, Sir Gawain,' said Bercilak in high good humour. 'And what have you to give me in exchange?'

Without a word Gawain went up to his host and kissed him on the cheek. The two men laughed and slapped each other on the back and arm in arm went in to dinner. They drank several flagons of wine and agreed that on the following day they would repeat the bargain.

So, the next morning, as on the one before, the lord of the castle left early for the hunt, and his lady came to Gawain's bedroom. Again she sat down on the bed.

'Well, Sir Gawain, have you already forgotten what passed between us yesterday? Are you not going to claim your kiss?'

Gawain blushed. 'I dared not ask,' he said, 'lest you should refuse me.' Then he kissed her and the two of them flirted and talked until it was time for Mass.

In the evening Bercilak returned, this time with a wild boar which he had brought down after a furious chase. Proudly he showed off its size and strength and boasted of the difficulty of its capture. Gawain listened admiringly and then, as before, gave his host a kiss on the cheek. Again the evening was spent in feasting and merriment, with a concert of Christmas carols during which the lady stared at Gawain shamelessly. Gawain pretended not to notice.

On the third day, New Year's Eve, Bercilak left at dawn with his troop of horsemen while Gawain slept heavily until awakened by the lady. She looked prettier than ever in a thin dress trimmed with fur and jewels, cut very low at front and back. Running into the room, she flung open the window, drew back the curtains of the bed, and kissed him playfully. 'What a lazy man you are!' she cried, shaking him by the shoulder.

Gawain groaned and forced open his eyes. When he saw how lovely she was, and how ardently she gazed at him, he was gravely tempted to betray his trust.

'Come, sir,' said the lady, taking his hand. 'How can you resist me – unless of course there is some other lady to whom you have given your heart?'

'There is no one,' Gawain replied. 'Nor do I wish to fall in love for a while yet.'

'That is the worst answer of all,' she said crossly, withdrawing her hand. 'I see there is no hope for me, so I shall leave you in peace. But before I go, let me have something to remember you by. Let me have your glove so that I may keep it with me after you have gone, and by looking at it recall the happy days we spent together. You cannot refuse me so small a thing.'

'Alas, you deserve a richer token than I can give you. I came here on a quest. I brought nothing with me except my horse and the clothes on my back. I have neither jewels nor gold. Truly, madam, it grieves me deeply that I have nothing worthy of you.'

'Then I shall give *you* something.' She drew from her finger a gold ring set with diamonds.

'No, indeed, madam,' said Gawain gently. 'I could not accept so valuable a gift.'

The lady sighed. 'If you think my ring too costly, then, Sir Gawain, will you take this girdle? You need have no scruple about accepting that.'

And she untied from her waist a green silk girdle with a golden fringe. 'Any man who wears this magic belt will be kept safe from all harm.'

At that moment it occurred to Gawain that if this were true, he could not be hurt by the Knight of the Green Chapel. So he agreed to take it, and as she put it into his hands, she kissed him and made him promise not to tell her husband.

When Bercilak returned that evening Gawain, resplendent in a turquoise surcoat trimmed with ermine, went to meet him. Putting his arms around him, he kissed him on both cheeks.

'I am afraid I have little to offer in return,' said Bercilak. 'All I found today was this,' and he threw on the floor the stiffened corpse of a little shabby fox.

Then the whole company spent a roistering evening, singing songs and telling stories, and Gawain again thanked his host for all his hospitality. They embraced in pledge of their friendship, and before parting for the night, Bercilak promised to send a servant to accompany Gawain to the Green Chapel.

The next morning was overcast and cold. The wind whistled from the hills and snow fell in freezing drifts. Shivering in the grey dawn, Gawain dressed quickly, being careful to tie the silk girdle about his waist. He mounted Gringolet and clattered over the drawbridge, followed by his guide.

The two men rode in silence through the icy woods until the guide stopped suddenly. 'Sir Gawain, we are almost at the Green Chapel, but I implore you not to go further. This is a wild and dangerous place and the Green Knight is a terrible man. He has the strength of five and is a savage killer. Few men meet him and live to tell the tale. To continue on this path means certain death.'

'I am grateful for your warning,' replied Gawain coldly, 'but I am no coward. There is no power on earth that will keep me from my encounter at the Green Chapel.'

'So be it,' said the guide. 'Here is your helmet and your lance. If you follow the narrow track between those rocks, you will come to the Chapel.'

Gawain spurred on Gringolet, riding right down into the ravine, but he saw no sign of any dwelling, only great jagged boulders rising up on either side. Then he caught sight of a little grass-covered mound. 'Is this what I am looking for?' he thought, dismounting to examine it more closely. It seemed deserted, a small evil-looking hummock with an opening at either end. As Gawain walked round it, he heard a whirring, rushing noise coming at him from all sides.

'Who's there?' cried Gawain, startled.

'Stay where you are! And stand to receive the blow which I promised you.' With these words the Green Knight appeared on the top of the hummock, whirling round his head a great axe, its shining blade honed to a deadly edge.

'Welcome, Sir Gawain,' said the Knight, descending the hummock. 'I see you are a man of your word. Remove your helmet. It is my turn to take aim at you.'

Obediently Gawain took off his helmet and knelt before the Knight, his head bowed. With all his strength, the Green Knight brought the axe whistling down, but just in time Gawain shrank slightly to one side so that the blade missed him by a hair.

'What!' bellowed the Knight. 'Are you afraid? I never flinched when I knelt before you. Surely you are not such a coward as to try to escape your due!'

'I shall not move the next time,' Gawain said penitently. 'If my head falls to the ground, I shall not flinch.'

'Have at you then!' cried the Knight fiercely, brandishing his axe and making as if to bring it down. But at the last second he held back. 'Now I shall put to the test the courage of one of King Arthur's famous knights. Now I shall see what kind of man you are.'

'Stop threatening me and strike your blow!' said Gawain angrily. 'You have my word I shall not flinch.'

So up went the axe and down it flashed on the white skin of Gawain's neck. Although savage, it was a glancing blow which caught him only on the side of his neck.

When Gawain saw the blood spurt on the snow, he jumped to his feet, snatching up his sword and shield. Never in his life had he felt so light of heart. 'Enough!' he cried. 'Our bargain is complete! You cannot touch me now!'

'Be calm,' replied the Knight. 'Our pact is concluded. Had I intended, I could have done you much greater harm. Twice I pretended to strike, and that was for the two evenings when you kept your word and made a true exchange, giving me the kisses my wife had given you. The third time I gave you a little cut to reprove you for concealing from me the silken girdle you have about your waist. For I know it all, all your flirtation and kissing, for it was I who set my wife to test you. I sent her to see if you were in truth a perfect Knight. But your faith was flawed. You broke your word.'

Gawain stood as though stunned, and the blood rushed to his face. 'I have betrayed the code of chivalry. I am not worthy to be called Knight,' he said bitterly, in an agony of shame. Tugging loose the girdle, he flung it to the ground and turned to go.

But the Knight laughed and held him back. 'No, Gawain, you have done penance by withstanding my blow. You have confessed your guilt and now you are as pure as if you had never been at fault. As for the girdle,' he picked it up and held it out. 'Accept it as a gift from me. Wear it as a token of your trial.'

'I thank you, sir,' said Gawain with dignity. 'I will take the girdle as a reminder of my frailty. Should I be tempted to be proud, one look at this will humble me again. And now I have a last favour to ask you – that you tell me your name and who you are.'

'I am Bercilak of Haut Desert. I am in the power of Morgan the Fay, whose witchcraft transforms me into the Green Knight whom you see before you now. She it was who sent me to Camelot to challenge the renown of the Round Table. She is the old woman you saw accompanying my wife.'

Then Bercilak begged Gawain to return with him to his castle, but Gawain refused, thanking him for his kindness. He set off for Camelot, the green girdle tied across his breastplate for everyone to see.

Arthur and Guinevere and all their court welcomed him joyfully, eager to hear the full account of his adventure. Gawain left out nothing, and when he finished, Arthur praised him and decreed that every knight present should wear a green silken girdle as a badge of the highest honour and purity of heart.

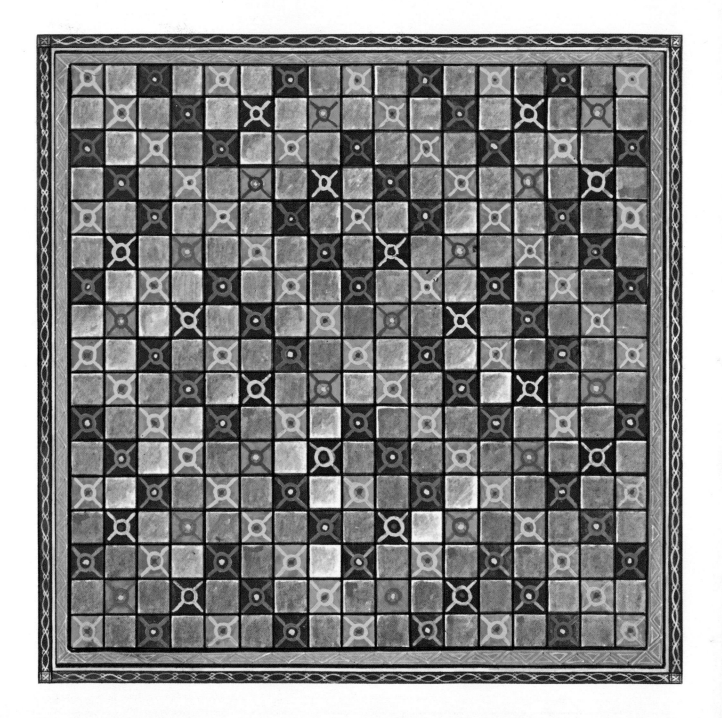